T0418309

FRENCH BULLDOGS

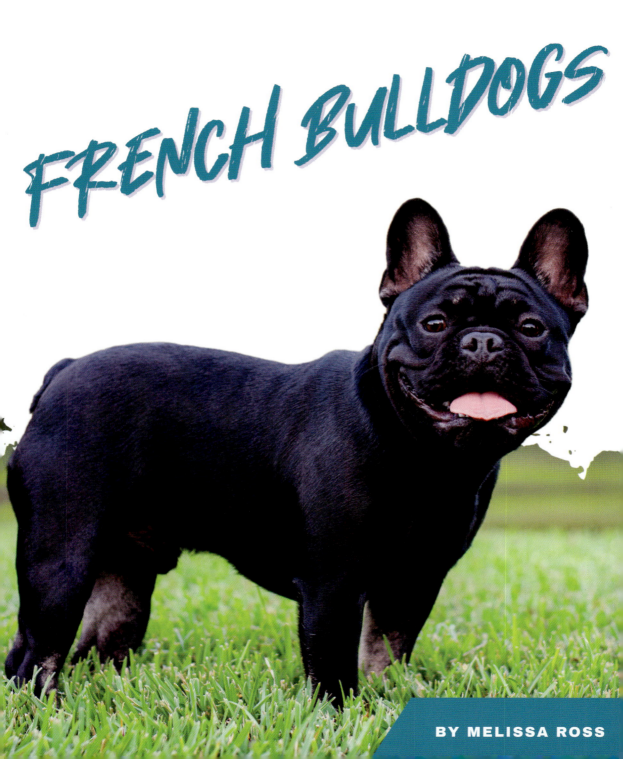

BY MELISSA ROSS

Apex is distributed by North Star Editions:
sales@northstareditions.com | 888-417-0195

Produced for Apex by Red Line Editorial.

Photographs ©: Shutterstock Images, cover, 1, 4–5, 6, 7, 8–9, 10–11, 12, 14–15, 16–17, 18, 20–21, 22–23, 24, 25, 26–27, 29; Adoc-Photos/Corbis Historical/Getty Images, 13

Library of Congress Control Number: 2023921785

ISBN
978-1-63738-908-9 (hardcover)
978-1-63738-948-5 (paperback)
979-8-89250-045-6 (ebook pdf)
979-8-89250-006-7 (hosted ebook)

Printed in the United States of America
Mankato, MN
082024

NOTE TO PARENTS AND EDUCATORS

Apex books are designed to build literacy skills in striving readers. Exciting, high-interest content attracts and holds readers' attention. The text is carefully leveled to allow students to achieve success quickly. Additional features, such as bolded glossary words for difficult terms, help build comprehension.

TABLE OF CONTENTS

CHAPTER 1

CITY DOG

AFrench bulldog sees his owner grab a leash. The dog gets excited. He runs to the door. The owner clips the leash to the dog's collar. They go for a walk.

Owners should use leashes when walking dogs, especially in busy cities.

Dogs living in cities can get exercise at dog parks.

Many people pass them on the sidewalk. Tall buildings rise up on either side. Eventually, they reach a dog park.

APARTMENT LIVING

French bulldogs are small dogs. They don't need a lot of space. They also don't bark very often. So, they make great pets for apartments.

Some apartments allow only small dogs.

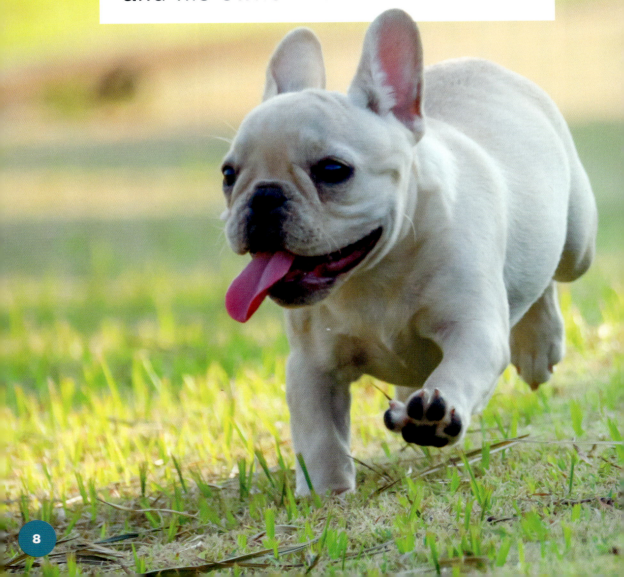

Another dog is at the park, too. The two dogs play for a while. Then the French bulldog and his owner walk back home.

FAST FACT

French bulldogs are social. They get along well with people and other pets.

French bulldogs are often friendly and playful.

CHAPTER 2

FRENCH BULLDOG HISTORY

Early bulldogs came from England. They were medium sized. But in the 1800s, people bred English bulldogs to be smaller. The little dogs became **popular** with English **lacemakers**.

English bulldogs are strong dogs. They weigh 40 to 50 pounds (18 to 23 kg).

A French bulldog (front) has bigger ears and fewer wrinkles than an English bulldog.

Many of the lacemakers moved to France by the 1860s. They took their bulldogs with them. The small dogs mixed with local dogs in France. They formed a new **breed**.

FANCY FRENCHIE

In the late 1800s, many people wanted French bulldogs. However, the dogs cost a lot of money. So, mainly wealthy people owned them.

Many people living in Paris, France, owned French bulldogs.

Many Americans visited France in the late 1800s. Some brought bulldogs home with them. The dogs became common pets in other countries, too.

FAST FACT

In 2022, French bulldogs were the most popular dog breed in the United States.

French bulldogs tend to be calm. They are easy for owners to take many places.

CHAPTER 3

SMALL BULLDOG BODY

French bulldogs are short and strong. They stand 11 to 13 inches (28 to 33 cm) tall. They weigh up to 28 pounds (13 kg).

Even though they are small, French bulldogs have strong muscles.

French bulldogs have square heads and **broad** faces. They have wrinkles above their noses. Their ears are large and pointed.

FLAT FACES

Like all bulldogs, Frenchies have compressed snouts. Some people think the dogs' flat faces are cute. But their short noses and wrinkles can make it hard for them to breathe.

French bulldogs are known for their big, bat-like ears.

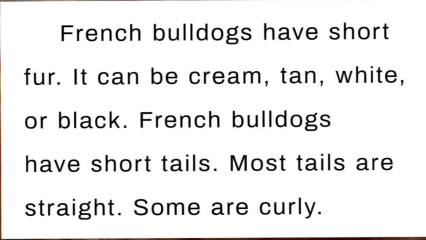

French bulldogs have short fur. It can be cream, tan, white, or black. French bulldogs have short tails. Most tails are straight. Some are curly.

FAST FACT

Frenchies get cold easily. They may need to wear coats in winter.

A coat can help a French bulldog stay warm in cold weather.

CHAPTER 4

FRENCH BULLDOG CARE

French bulldogs need weekly brushing. Their faces need cleaning, too. Dirt gets trapped in their wrinkles. Owners should clean the folds with a damp cloth and then dry them.

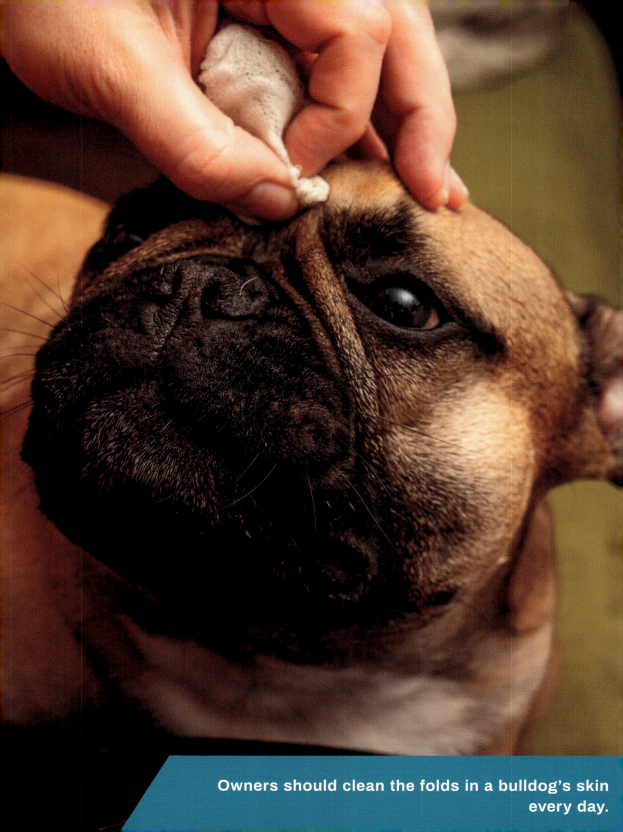

Owners should clean the folds in a bulldog's skin every day.

French bulldogs may bark if left alone for a long time.

French bulldogs don't need very much exercise. But they require lots of attention. They don't like to be left alone for too long.

STAY COOL

French bulldogs **overheat** easily. Dogs cool down by panting. But Frenchies can't pant as easily because of their short snouts. So, the dogs shouldn't be outside for long on hot days.

Owners should make sure Frenchies don't overheat. That can happen if the dogs exercise too much.

Consistent training is important for French bulldogs. The dogs can be **stubborn**. They do not always listen. But most are eager to please their owners.

FAST FACT

Giving dogs treats or other **rewards** can help with training.

With the right training, French bulldogs can learn many tricks.

COMPREHENSION QUESTIONS

Write your answers on a separate piece of paper.

1. Write a few sentences explaining the main ideas of Chapter 2.

2. Would you like to have a French bulldog for a pet? Why or why not?

3. How much do French bulldogs typically weigh?
   A. less than 13 pounds (6 kg)
   B. up to 28 pounds (13 kg)
   C. more than 33 pounds (15 kg)

4. Why would people in apartments want dogs that don't bark much?
   A. because apartments never allow pets
   B. so the dogs don't need to go for walks
   C. so the dogs don't bother nearby people

5. What does **wealthy** mean in this book?

*However, the dogs cost a lot of money. So, mainly **wealthy** people owned them.*

    A. rich

    B. sad

    C. young

6. What does **compressed** mean in this book?

*Like all bulldogs, Frenchies have **compressed** snouts. Some people think the dogs' flat faces are cute.*

    A. pressed in

    B. long and thin

    C. falling apart

Answer key on page 32.

GLOSSARY

breed
A specific type of dog that has its own look and abilities.

broad
Wide.

consistent
Done the same way over and over.

lacemakers
People who make lace, a fragile fabric that decorates clothing.

overheat
To become too hot.

popular
Liked by or known to many people.

rewards
Things given in return for good work.

snouts
The noses and mouths of animals.

stubborn
Not willing to change how one thinks or acts.

BOOKS

Aboff, Marcie. *Fast Facts About French Bulldogs*. North Mankato, MN: Capstone Press, 2021.

Noll, Elizabeth. *Toy Dogs*. Minneapolis: Bellwether Media, 2021.

Pearson, Marie. *Dogs*. Mankato, MN: The Child's World, 2020.

ONLINE RESOURCES

Visit **www.apexeditions.com** to find links and resources related to this title.

ABOUT THE AUTHOR

Melissa Ross is the author of educational books for children, including *Forensics for Kids*. In her spare time, she enjoys spending time with family, drawing, and going on walks with her dog.

INDEX

ANSWER KEY:
1. Answers will vary; 2. Answers will vary; 3. B; 4. C; 5. A; 6. A